Why do puppies chew?

camilla de la Bedoyere

Miles Kelly

D1122258

First published in 2011 by Miles Kelly Publishing Ltd
Harding's Barn, Bardfield End Green, Thaxted,
Essex, CM6 3PX, UK

2 4 6 8 10 9 7 5 3 1

Publishing Director Belinda Gallagher
Creative Director Jo Cowan
Editorial Director Rosie McGuire
Editor Claire Philip
Volume Designer Andrea Slane
Cover Designer Kayleigh Allen
Image Manager Liberty Newton
Indexer Gill Lee
Production Manager Elizabeth Collins
Reprographics Anthony Cambray,
Stephan Davis, Ian Paulyn

ISBN 978-1-84810-452-5

Printed in China

British Library Cataloguing-in-Publication Data

A catalogue record for this book is
available from the British Library

ACKNOWLEDGEMENTS
The publishers would like to thank the following
artists who have contributed to this book:
Ian Jackson (cover), Mike Foster (character cartoons)
All other artwork from the Miles Kelly Artwork Bank

The publishers would like to thank the following
sources for the use of their photographs:

Dreamstime.com 8 & 30(tr) Lilun
Fotolia.com 12 jsatt83; 13(b) & 30(cr) Carola Schubbel
iStockphoto.com 18 David Schliepp
Rex Features 13(t) c.W. Disney/Everet
Shutterstock.com Back cover daniel budiman;
11 plavevski; 23 Marcel Jancovic; 29 aspen rock

All other photographs are from:
Corel, digitalSTOCK, ImageState, PhotoDisc

Every effort has been made to acknowledge the
source and copyright holder of each picture. Miles Kelly
Publishing apologises for any unintentional errors or
omissions.

Made with paper from a sustainable forest

www.mileskelly.net
info@mileskelly.net

www.factsforprojects.com

Self-publish your
children's book

buddingpress.co.uk

Contents

Are dogs and puppies friendly?

Most pet dogs and puppies are tame – this means they are friendly and like to be around people. There are more than 200 types, or breeds, of dogs such as pointers, which are clever and easily trained.

Pointer puppies

what do dogs eat?

Newborn puppies drink their mother's milk. As they get older, dogs eat meat and special biscuits. Their food contains vitamins that help them grow strong and healthy. Dogs need plenty of fresh water every day.

Burmese mountain dog

Dog biscuits

Chew

Fresh water

messy pup!

Some dogs love to get mucky. They'll roll around in stinky mud or jump into dirty water for a quick dip!

Yorkshire Terrier

Do toy dogs love to play?

Toy dogs are small dogs. They love to play with children who hold them carefully and treat them well. Yorkshire Terriers (also known as Yorkies), Chihuahuas and Pugs are toy dogs and they make great family pets.

Measure

Some toy dogs are only 20 centimetres tall. Use a ruler to find out how big this is.

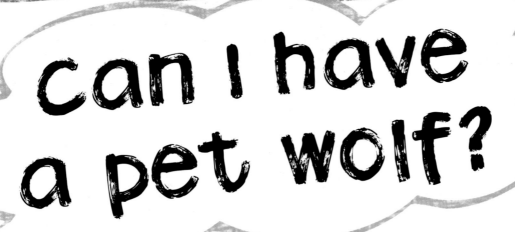

can I have a pet wolf?

No – it would be too dangerous! Wolves are the largest type of wild dog, and they aren't tame. Grey wolves live in family groups called packs that hunt together and look for animals to eat.

Grey wolf mother and cubs

Are all baby dogs called puppies?

No, young wild dogs such as dingoes and foxes are called cubs. Dingoes live in Australia and foxes, such as the red fox, live in many parts of the world.

Fox cub

Itchy and scratchy!

Tiny jumping bugs called fleas can set up home in a dog's fur. Fleas make dogs itch, so they scratch.

Think

When people come to your home, how does your family make them feel welcome?

Why are postmen scared of dogs?

A dog likes to guard its home, or territory, so if a stranger, such as a postman, comes into its territory a dog might bark. Not all dogs bark as a warning — sometimes they are just happy to see you!

what is a litter?

'Litter' is the word for a group of puppies born at the same time. A mother dog is usually pregnant for about two months, as the puppies grow inside her. Most mother dogs have litters of three to eight puppies at a time and take care of them for the first few weeks of their lives.

Paint
Draw your family and some dogs that look like them. Then add colour with paints.

Mother dog

Are dogs helpful?

Dogs can help people in many ways. Guide dogs are trained to help people who have difficulty seeing, hearing or walking. These dogs can warn their owners of danger and guide them safely when they go out.

Mum
Cavalier King
Charles Spaniel

Puppy

Dad
German
Spitz

Do all puppies look like their parents?

Not if the mother and father dog are different breeds. Puppies may have features from both parents – long ears from their Mum, for example, and fluffy fur from their Dad.

Litter of Dachshund puppies

Dogs in space!

In 1960, two dogs called Strelka and Belka were sent into space by astronauts – they landed home safely.

How smart are dogs?

Border collie

Some dogs are much smarter than others. The cleverest dogs can be trained to work with people. Collies are trained to herd sheep on farms. They also protect the sheep from animals that might hunt them, such as foxes.

can dogs and puppies swim?

Some puppies learn to swim as soon as they can run, while others never learn. When dogs and puppies swim, they move as though they are running underwater – this is known as the doggy paddle.

Alaskan malamute

Swim

When you next go swimming, practise doing the doggy paddle.

soggy doggy!

Basset hounds find swimming in water very difficult because they have such short legs!

Do dogs look like their owners?

That's a matter of opinion! It is true that some tall, thin people own dogs that are long and thin – and some short, broad people have short, broad dogs. However, most dogs and their owners look very different from one another.

why do dogs chase balls?

It is natural for dogs to chase things that move, especially balls. They do this because pet dogs are related to wild dogs, which have to catch food to eat. Dogs are playful animals too, and chasing balls is fun!

Dog chasing a ball

what's up!

Healthy dogs have much better hearing than humans. They react to sounds that are very far away.

can dogs have stripes?

Dogs come in many colours, but none have stripes!
Dalmatians are known for their white coats and
black spots. The puppies are born completely white –
their spots develop after a few weeks.

Walt Disney's
101 Dalmatians

Do old dogs turn grey?

Yes – the fur around their muzzles turns
grey or white. Some elderly dogs also
have hearing problems. Old dogs
have less energy than young puppies
and so they sleep
a lot more.

Paint

Draw a picture
of how you think
you will look
when you are
grown-up.

Elderly dog

How do dogs keep warm?

Saint Bernard

Most dogs have thick fur coats to keep out the cold. Saint Bernards are suited to very cold climates. They are large, strong dogs bred to rescue lost travellers in snowy mountains.

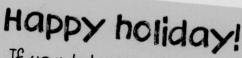

Happy holiday!
If you take a pet dog abroad they will need their own 'pet passport'. It shows they are fit and healthy.

Which puppies have wrinkles?

The wrinkliest puppies are Shar Peis. They have deep folds of skin around their heads, faces and bodies. As they get older, Shar Peis grow into their wrinkles, but even the adults are still very wrinkly around their heads.

Shar Pei puppies

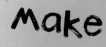

Make
Design a poster showing some animals that can survive in very cold places.

Are dogs colour-blind?

Dogs can see colours – but not in the same way we do. Guide dogs can't tell the difference between red, amber and green in a traffic light. They look at the brightness and position of a light to know when it is safe to cross.

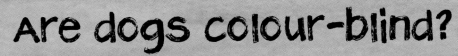

Why do puppies chew?

Puppies chew when they are teething (growing new teeth). It can make their gums sore and chewing helps them feel better. Dogs also like to chew toys when they are playing.

Labrador puppy

Why do dogs fetch?

Hunting dogs were trained to fetch game birds, such as pheasants, that had been caught by their owners whilst hunting. Now most of these types of dogs, such as retrievers, are kept as pets. They still love to play fetch!

Golden retriever

When is a dog like a sausage?

When it's a sausage dog! This type of dog has a very long body and four short legs. The proper name is 'Dachshund', which means 'badger dog'. Dachshunds are very good at digging.

Imagine
Make up a story about a sausage dog. What is its name, and what mischief does it get up to?

Top dog!
A long time ago, a dog ruled the country of Norway. It was king for three years and signed important papers with a paw print!

what is a rescue dog?

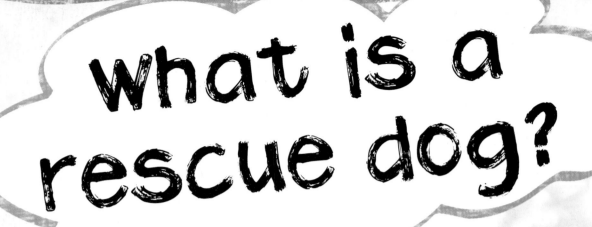

Rescue dogs are trained to find people who are lost or trapped. These dogs use their strong sense of smell to follow a person's trail. They can even find people who are trapped under snow.

Chow chow

Do all dogs have pink tongues?

Not all dogs – Chow Chows have blue-black tongues. The insides of their mouths are blue-black too. These dogs have been bred in China for thousands of years and are very loyal to their owners.

Alsatian
rescue dog

when can puppies wag their tails?

Puppies usually start to wag their tails when they are about four weeks old and still feeding on their mother's milk. Older dogs wag their tails when they are excited to see another dog, or a person they like.

Are puppies born blind?

Newborn puppies are born blind and totally helpless. They first open their eyes when they are about nine days old. At three weeks of age, puppies can move around clumsily. At six weeks old they begin to eat solid food.

Newborn puppy

Sloppy doggy!

When some dogs see a plate of food their mouths fill up with saliva, which sometimes dribbles out of their mouths. It's called 'drooling'.

Two weeks old

Three weeks old

How do hot dogs cool down?

Panting

Dogs pant when they need to cool down. When we get too hot we can sweat, and take off some clothes. Dogs can't take off their thick, warm fur and they can only sweat from their paws. Panting helps them keep cool and comfortable.

Talk

Ask your Mum or Dad about the ways you have changed since you were a baby.

Why do puppies sleep so much?

When puppies are awake they are busy learning, playing and feeding. It tires them out quickly. As they grow, puppies spend less time snoozing.

Five weeks old

Eight weeks old

Why do dogs love to sniff?

Dogs have a much better sense of smell than we do. They like to sniff things because smells, or scents, tell them a lot about the world around them. They can even recognize people and other dogs by their scents.

Basset hound

Pretend

Imagine you are following a trail. Use your eyes, ears and sense of smell to find your way.

can dogs sense danger?

Dogs often react to sudden movements or loud noises. It means they are alert to possible dangers. Some dogs can even sense earthquakes and thunderstorms before they happen.

Bad fur day!

The fur of Hungarian Puli dogs grows down to the ground. It needs brushing every day so it doesn't get too knotted.

Huskies pulling sleigh

which is the strongest dog?

Huskies are one of the strongest dog breeds. They live in cold places and are strong enough to cope with freezing weather while pulling heavy sleds.

Do dogs have haircuts?

Long-haired dogs need haircuts to keep them cool. It can be very dangerous for dogs to overheat and lots of fur keeps in warmth. Short-haired dogs shed their fur throughout the year, mostly in the spring and summer.

Chocolate poodles

can dogs talk to each other?

Dogs 'talk' to each other and to us by barking. Loud, non-stop barking usually means that a dog is worried about something. Two or three short barks are a dog's way of saying 'Hello'.

Brittany spaniel

Nice to meet you

Dogs and puppies are friendly creatures and can live alongside other pets happily – as long as they are properly introduced.

why do puppies need exercise?

Exercise is good for puppies and dogs. It keeps them healthy and strong, and uses up energy so they sleep well. Exercise is also a type of play, which makes dogs and puppies happy – without it they can become restless.

Exercise
Riding bikes and playing in parks are fun ways to get some exercise.

25

Do big ears help dogs hear?

Not if they are long and floppy, like a bloodhound's. These dogs have a fantastic sense of smell but their large, droopy ears can cause hearing problems and even deafness.

Bad breath!

Dogs can have bad breath and gum disease, just like us! Owners should brush their dog's teeth with toothpaste made specially for dogs.

Bloodhound

Do dogs like being brushed?

Some dogs like being brushed, but others hate it! Brushing a dog is called 'grooming' and it helps to keep their fur clean and tidy. Samoyeds have beautiful white coats, and most of them like their long, thick fur being brushed.

Samoyed

How big do dogs grow?

A dog's size depends on its breed. Some dogs, such as Great Danes, grow very tall and can measure more than 80 centimetres from the floor to their shoulder. Chihuahuas are one of the smallest breeds of dog. They can be just 15 centimetres tall.

Great Dane

Discover
Use a measuring tape to see how tall a Great Dane can be.

Chihuahua

can puppies be trained?

Cardboard box bed

Puppies are eager to learn, so they can be easily trained. As they grow, puppies learn to recognize their own names and how to follow commands. They also need to be house-trained, which means going outside to go to the toilet.

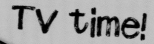

TV time!

Some dogs will sit and watch the bright lights and moving images on TV screens. They don't understand what they see, but seem to like it!

Do puppies go to the doctor?

Puppies need to see a vet if they are unwell. A vet is an animal doctor. All dogs and puppies need to visit the vet so they can be given vaccinations to keep them healthy.

Vet examining a puppy

Play
Pretend you are a vet, and you have a surgery full of unwell pets to look after.

Canis Minor

When is a dog a star?

When it is in the sky! Groups of stars are called constellations and two of them are named after dogs. One is called *Canis Major*, or Bigger Dog, and the other one is *Canis Minor*, or Smaller Dog.

Canis Major

Quiz time

Do you remember what you have read about dogs and puppies? Here are some questions to test your memory. The pictures will help you. If you get stuck, read the pages again.

3. What is a litter?

page 8

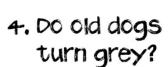

4. Do old dogs turn grey?

page 13

1. What do dogs eat?

page 5

5. Which puppies have wrinkles?

page 15

2. Why are postmen scared of dogs?

page 7

6. Are dogs colour-blind?

page 15

7. Why do puppies chew?

page 16

11. Can dogs talk to each other?

page 25

8. When can puppies wag their tails?

page 19

12. Can puppies be trained?

page 28

9. Are puppies born blind?

page 20

13. When is a dog a star?

page 29

10. Can dogs sense danger?

page 23

Answers

1. Meat and special biscuits
2. Because dogs bark to protect their territory
3. A group of puppies born at the same time
4. Yes, some fur turns grey or white
5. Shar Pei puppies
6. No, they just see colour differently to us
7. They chew because their gums are sore or during play
8. When they are around four weeks old
9. Yes, puppies only open their eyes when they are around nine days old
10. Yes, some even sense thunderstorms and earthquakes
11. Yes, but by barking – not with words
12. Yes, puppies are eager to learn
13. When it's a star constellation, such as *Canis Minor*

Index